GOD'S FOOTPRINT ON THE LAND

Uncovering, Discovering, and Recovering the Purposes of God

by

Alistair Petrie

Releasing The Kingdom of Heaven Series

CHI BOOKS

WHAT OTHERS ARE SAYING ABOUT THIS BOOK …

YES! Land can be healed! And this condensed version of Alistair Petrie's pioneering teaching will show you how. This outstanding summary of all the foundational principles, will guide you through a maze of potential issues in a clear, succinct and practical manner. I wish I'd had this book thirty years ago! Essential understanding for pastors, leaders, business executives and all land owners. Life-transforming truths packaged for immediate use!

Peter Horrobin

Founder and International Director, Ellel Ministries International – UK

God's Footprint on the Land provides revelation and understanding from the Scripture, which then can be realized through informed prayer to 'heal the land'.

Alistair Petrie provides an amazing journey through Scripture of 'theology of land' with practical examples of healing of the land.

As a First Nations leader and minister from the Piikani/Blackfoot Nation, I can attest to the effects of the work of repentance of four major iniquities in Scripture that defile the land; they are broken covenants, the shedding of innocent blood, sexual immorality, witchcraft and idolatry. We have witnessed the Lord providing a template for other First Nations in healing the land. I wholeheartedly recommend the wide distribution and reading of this series by Alistair.

Manfred North Peigan

Pastor, Piikani/Blackfoot Nation, Alberta – Canada

Land is important to the Lord. Having been taught the biblical principles outlined in this book by Dr Alistair Petrie and teaching the application of them in many nations in Africa, Asia and the Caucasus over the past fifteen years, I cannot recommend this book highly enough.

I have seen miracles of floods receding, rain returning to scorched land with crops flourishing, fatal accidents ceasing after black spots cleansed and land becoming extraordinarily fertile after repentance prayer. If we seek the revelation to apply the Lords blueprint to defiled land, this book which is wonderfully clear will assist us to bring healing to our nations.

Lieutenant Colonel (Retired), Jan Ransom MBE

Director Flame International – UK

I don't remember hearing a message about how important the land is to God and the connection between it and the move of God or lack thereof. But that was changed when I first heard Alistair Petrie teach on the subject using much Scripture and examples from today. Once you understand the spiritual history of the land to everyday life, you can begin to understand why certain things happen – and how to minister to the issues of the land in order to free it for God's blessing. I highly recommend *God's Footprint on the Land*. You will find a treasure of information that will help you deal with many issues that you never realised were connected to the land.

Dr Ruth Ruibal
President, Julio C. Ruibal Ministries – Columbia

God not only made the earth but created mankind from His dirt. Unfortunately many of us don't know whose dirt it is. The Bible clearly states that we are custodians of the land. I have spent most of my seventy-eight years with indigenous people in Australia and other nations. During this time I have seen a very deep relationship between indigenous people and the land where God has placed them. In this short but insightful book you will discover the redemptive keys that will help you become a more effective custodian of the land.

As *God's Footprint on the Land* suggests, we need to grasp afresh that God intends us to be part of the restoration and healing of the land in order to bring it back to His original intention and purpose. He has placed us on His earth so that He could bless us through His land, however the land is sick, so God is unable to fully bless us as He intended.

Alistair expounds clearly from Scripture what actually makes the land sick, providing insightful, practical and proven processes in how it can be healed so that God can bless both the land and its people. I encourage you to take seriously the principles that Alistair has outlined and prayerfully learn how to apply them on the land where you are God's custodian, wherever that might be.

Rev. John Blacket
Perth, Western Australia – Australia

BY THE SAME AUTHOR

GOD'S DESIGN FOR CHALLENGING TIMES
Discovering Freedom in an Age of Compromise

IN HOLY FEAR
Rediscovering the Fear of the Lord

PROPHETIC DITCH DIGGING
Preparing For Breakthrough

GOD'S FOOTPRINT IN BUSINESS
Bringing Transformation to the Marketplace

Above CHI-Books titles available worldwide from online suppliers including:
www.amazon.com | www.koorong.com.au | www.bookdepository.co.uk |
www.partnershipministries.org

eBooks available from: Amazon Kindle | Apple iBookstore |
Barnes & Noble | Chapters | Koorong.com

TRANSFORMED! PEOPLES – CITIES – NATIONS
10 Principles for Sustaining Genuine Revival

Sovereign World Ltd, Lancaster, 2003: Republished 2008, Sovereign World Ltd

RELEASING HEAVEN ON EARTH

Grand Rapids, MI: Chosen Books, 2000: Republished 2008, Sovereign World Ltd

CHI–Books,
PO Box 6462, Upper Mt Gravatt,
Brisbane, QLD 4122, Australia

www.chibooks.org
publisher@chibooks.org

God's Footprint on the Land – *Uncovering, Discovering, and Recovering the Purposes of God*
Copyright © 2020 by Rev. Dr Alistair Petrie
Print ISBN: 978-0-6485108-5-7
eBook ISBN: 978-0-6485108-6-4

Printed in Australia, United Kingdom and the United States of America.

Distributed in the USA and internationally by Ingram Book Group and Amazon. Also available from: Bookdepository.co.uk and other outlets like Koorong.com in Australia.

Distribution of eBook version: Amazon Kindle, Apple iBooks, Koorong. com and others like Barnes & Noble NOOK and KOBO.

CHI-Books is the publishing imprint of CityHarvest International

Editorial assistance: Anne Hamilton
Cover design: Dave Stone
Layout: Jonathan Gould

ABOUT THE SERIES

In spite of the challenges we face in this day and age, we are also witnessing a move of God on an unprecedented global scale. This book is the third in a series that will enable us to connect to this worldwide move of God as we address the whole subject of land — man — and God. In the overall series we will illustrate specific and targeted types of prayer from Scriptural as well as missional activity that will give us tools for breakthrough and change.

Over many decades of involvement in prayer and on-the-ground initiatives within the global arena, we have repeatedly found the main challenge to be frustration, despair and not knowing how to obtain breakthroughs in seemingly impossible situations.

You will discover in this series wisdom and insight into a number of thrilling forms of prayer strategy God has given to His church. These are strategies that underline the promise of Luke 1:37 that indeed, nothing is impossible with God!

First book in this series: *Prophetic Ditch Digging—Preparing For Breakthrough.*

Second in this series: *God's Footprint in Business—Bringing Transformation to the Marketplace.*

CONTENTS

FOREWORD

Alistair Petrie's original work, *Releasing Heaven on Earth*, has been a key reference work for our ministry in understanding theology of the land concepts. This insightful book has served as a valuable resource in establishing a valid biblical base for strategic prayer with a focus on healing of the land.

In *God's Footprint on the Land*, Alistair adds to his earlier work, by refining the essential concepts and principles that contribute to seeing God fulfill His promise to heal the land. Each chapter provides vital information that helps the Body of Christ see and to understand key components that are essential for success in carrying out land healing prayer.

In our ministry we have applied Alistair's principles and witnessed amazing results. Like him, we have seen dark powers flee as God's presence comes to visit the land, changing lives and bringing significant environmental change. It is one thing to talk about biblical concepts, but it is quite another to actually see God transform dire situations when His people choose to act upon the divine instructions outlined in His word.

I believe the biblically informed material presented in this book will enable church, business and the marketplace leaders to secure the land they intend to establish their organization on. They will quickly discern the key spiritual obstacles that may be hindering their progress and prosperity. It will enable the reader to build a workable 'healing of the land' template and informed prayer strategy.

God's Footprint on the Land is a must read for those desiring kingdom breakthrough; those seeking to see the transforming power of God's presence permeate their efforts. This book will now become essential reading for all students who come to our prayer training courses or workshops.

We therefore highly recommend that you make this well thought-out guide first choice in your preparation for breakthrough, healing of the land prayer.

Dr Ivan and Dr Linda Doxtator
Executive Directors – First Nations Restoration Ministries

INTRODUCTION

Early on in our ministry days, God gave us an insight into a key principle that would forever form and fashion the decades of ministry that would follow both locally and globally. Our first book—*Releasing Heaven On Earth*—now long out of print—provided a detailed account into this principle, utilizing both Biblical and practical insights into the **theology of land**.

Understanding land from God's perspective requires a shift in our worldview, yet at the same time we found it became the key for breakthrough in literally hundreds of ministry initiatives we have conducted in many parts of the world in both local church and missional contexts.

In an abbreviated and updated version, with fresh and inspiring examples, and after repeated requests for this information, *God's Footprint on the Land* is now here!

As the subheading indicates, it is all about *"Uncovering — Discovering — and Recovering"* the healing and breakthrough purposes of God in our assigned areas of life and work and worship.

The first half of 2020 became one of the watershed moments of modern human history in that the Covid-19 virus virtually closed down planet Earth! Everything changed from the workplace — to education — to politics — and even how we could function as the church. As a ministry, we began fielding many new enquires concerning the relationship between sin in society that may affect the land upon which we live and work, especially in the area of plagues and disasters. Is there a connection? What does the Word of God say about this? Is there a directive from God for us to review and acknowledge, during such a time as this?

Isaiah 62:10 summarizes this perfectly —

> *"Pass through, pass through the gates! Prepare the way for the people. Build up, build up the highway! Remove the stones. Raise a banner for the nations."*

CHAPTER 1
What on Earth?

After arriving at our new church, it was clear something was definitely wrong. For months I had been teaching and preaching on solid Gospel topics, but we saw minimal change. It was a small church numerically when we arrived, with very few young families. It was therefore a church that had its funding underwritten by the denominational headquarters. But it was as if something had made the people in the area resistant to the Gospel and as if they were not even aware our church existed. We tried all sorts of publicity and visitation, but other than an occasional response, it was as if the overall area was spiritually blind and deaf to anything connected to the Gospel. I remember crying out to God — *"What on earth is going on here for heaven's sake?"*

Stones — Obstacles — and Land!
Years before, while training at theological college, the Lord had spoken certain things to us about our call to the ministry and He spoke from these verses in Isaiah that later would shape what He had in store for us:

"But whoever takes refuge in Me will inherit the land and possess My holy mountain." And it will be said: "Build up, build up, prepare the road! Remove the obstacles out of the way of My people." (Isaiah 57:13–14)

"Pass through, pass through the gates! Prepare the way for the people. Build up, build up the highway! Remove the stones. Raise a banner for the nations." (Isaiah 62:10)

Having now pastored in two very different but exciting church expressions in those years since college, we were asking God what exactly was going on in this new work. It was then He reminded us of those verses He had given years before.

Then, a third passage hit me between the eyes — Matthew 13:1–13 — the well-known Parable of the Sower. I knew the passage well — but not in the way God was now explaining it to us. I had always believed those birds that stole the seed sown by the farmer represented normal issues of disbelief that we would encounter in ministry. But what about those rocky places amidst shallow soil that prevented solid nurture and stability for the plants when they began to grow? What about the thorns which choked the plants from maturing? Surely, though, the passage meant that, if we were faithful, at least we would have some type of harvest from all our labour! Was that not what ministry involved?

However, the challenge was this — *"Still other seed fell on good soil, where it produced a crop — a hundred, sixty or thirty times what was sown. Whoever has ears, let Him hear."* (Matthew 13:8–9) Suddenly it was clear that God was challenging me with a different perspective on this entire passage — **one that would hold the key to opening up the spiritual eyesight of our community**!

What was God meaning? He reminded me of my family background — the farming side. It was normal for the family to walk the land every spring and remove stones and weeds before the farmer could sow the seeds. Why did we do this? Soil is always moving due to the rotation of the earth on its axis — thus new weeds and impediments were coming to the surface from deep places we had not dealt with the year before.

Then came a fourth passage that is both well-known but often misunderstood in its relationship to addressing obstacles, weeds and stones —

> *"If My people, who are called by My name, will humble themselves and pray and seek My face and turn from their wicked ways, then will I hear from heaven and will forgive their sin and will heal their land. Now My eyes will be open and My ears attentive to the prayers offered in this place. I have chosen and consecrated this temple so that My Name may be there forever. My eyes and My heart will always be there."* (2 Chronicles 7:14–16)

Removing stones, weeds and other sorts of obstacles — preparing a road — a highway — expecting a more productive harvest — and land being healed. God had caught my attention! There was a dimension to removing obstacles that was to be applied spiritually as well as physically. Impediments had to be removed if the seed, spiritual and physical, was to germinate properly and produce a harvest.

God was beginning to show us why we had experienced little breakthrough in our area. He was teaching us that we can pray for our communities in the same way that we address issues in the lives of people. But it would require having deeper insight and understanding than what we had experienced before.

A Call for Help

On one occasion we were contacted by a family who were mature Christians. After purchasing a new property, they had begun to experience serious issues that "normal prayer" had not alleviated. As a family they were now at odds with each other — the parents — the children — the entire household! Arguments and unacceptable behaviour were on the increase. The family pets were erratic in their behaviour, as were the livestock in their small holding. It was as if their being on this piece of land had activated many previously unseen issues and a restlessness and sense of hostility had been released. The productivity of both the livestock and the land itself was literally dying, and the members of the family were becoming increasingly ill. It was time to undertake some detailed research about the land.

In so doing we found there had been a history of violence and murder on this land. Traumatic events had blocked fruitfulness for both the land and the people who lived there.

After prayer and repentance for past and present issues which had occurred on this land, the change was astonishing. Family relationships were healed and restored at all levels, the erratic behaviour of the household pets and the farmyard animals ceased almost immediately, and the productivity on the land itself began to flourish. What had been dying was now bearing fruit. An immense peace and sense of welcome settled over the entire property. God was showing us what healing the land was all about.

Land could be "healed" in the same way as people — once the issues prohibiting the healing had been identified and addressed. Scripture even refers to us as being God's field (see 1 Corinthians 3:9) and so there are similarities between people being healed and land being healed!

CHAPTER 2
God — Man — and Land

God is Jealous for His land

Circumstances have varied greatly in our hundreds of experiences with the land over many years. But a consistent feature is that, once the spiritual "stones and obstacles" have been identified and removed, and then the people and the land have been consecrated for God's purposes, tangible healing and transformation has taken place. The promise of 2 Chronicles 7:14–16 has remained consistent, and the truth of Joel 2:18 has never shifted —

> "Then the Lord will be jealous for His land and took pity on His people."

The Psalmist was clear on this point —

> "The earth is the Lord's and everything in it, the world and all who live in it..." (Psalm 24:1)

> "The heavens are Yours, and Yours also the earth; You founded the world and all that is in it." (Psalm 89:11)

The Land is Mine

Genesis teaches us that God created land first, and then He created man to steward the land and His creation (cf. Genesis 1:9–28).

"The land must not be sold permanently, because the land is Mine and you reside in My land as foreigners and strangers. Throughout the land that you hold as a possession, you must provide for the redemption of the land." (Leviticus 25:23–24)

However, due to man's sin, the land — the ground — became cursed resulting in hostility and separation between God and man.

> *"Cursed is the ground because of you; through painful toil you will eat food from all the days of your life. It will produce thorns and thistles for you, and you will eat the plants of the field. By the sweat of your brow you will eat your food until you return to the ground..."* (Genesis 3:17–19)

Man continued to sin in his relationship and responsibility before God, leading to the murder of Abel by his brother Cain (Genesis 4:10). His on-going disobedience resulted in **serious consequences** at every level of life (see Deuteronomy 28:15–68). In Leviticus 26:32, God states, *"I Myself will lay waste the land..."*

Land is cursed when the Presence and purpose of God is rejected. It can be healed whenever and wherever His Presence returns.

These consequences — (which we will discuss later in chapter 5)—reflect the state of humanity when the love of God and His purposes for His people are rejected by His people, and His Presence is no longer in their midst. God's promises of provision, direction, and protection as well as the Power of His Presence in their midst, become **forfeited** due to the unholy worship and lifestyle the people have chosen in opposition to the purposes of God.

Simply put, land — ground — is cursed when the Presence and purpose of God is rejected. However, it can be made holy again (healed) whenever and wherever His Presence returns. That is the powerful promise repeated through Scripture!

Land Holds the Key

Understanding land from God's perspective is key if we want to see sustainable healing and transformation in our midst. Scripture explains that land contains the product of blessing and curse from previous years and generations. In essence it is a "feeding trough" or conduit for whatever takes place on any piece of property and its productivity in both present and future generations. It is the responsibility of the occupants or stewards of that property to address any issues past or present that cause any form of spiritual malaise or lack of productivity. Until this is addressed, the "product" of that land is subject to robbery, exploitation and the absence of God's Presence. This will affect every level of life, productivity, and vision in that area.

Putting it another way, the land represents God's "opinion" of things. It gives us clues, and enables us to learn through research and prayer, just *why* things are the way they are — *how* they got that way — *what* lies behind the attributes that may be unique to a particular city — and the *strategy* required to remedy the situation. Hosea 4:1–6 gives a graphic insight into the "mourning" of land due to issues that have taken place upon the land —

> "There is no faithfulness, no love, no acknowledgment of God in the land.

There is only cursing, lying and murder, stealing and adultery; they break all bounds, and bloodshed follows bloodshed. Because of this the land mourns."

No wonder the farmers despair with limited expectancy of harvest coming from the land (see also Joel 1:8–12). But this can be changed when people return to the Lord and address issues in their lives and communities that prohibit the harvest of people and land.

Amos 9:13–14 is quite clear on the promise of restoration —

"The days are coming," declares the Lord, "when the reaper will be overtaken by the plowman and the planter by the one treading grapes. New wine will drip from the mountains and flow from all the hills... they will plant vineyards and drink their wine; they will make gardens and eat their fruit.'"

Scripture has many promises such as this when it comes to the "healing of land". The word "land" (ground) is used 1717 times in Scripture. Repeatedly we learn that God is jealous for His land and wants nothing less than His highest purpose for His people; to experience the fruit that comes from all activity and from all productivity upon the land. He wants nothing to separate us from His Presence since, where His Presence dwells, there will be breakthrough and change.

The challenge for us is in understanding this concept of "land" from God's perspective. In order to understand the cause-and-effect of why sin committed on the land gives the enemy access and leverage to an area, we need to grasp the close connection between the spiritual and physical realms. We need a healthy, Biblical worldview!

CHAPTER 3
Having a 20–20 Worldview Vision

Land and World

The clue for us is that the words **land** and **world** do not mean the same — even though we tend to use them similarly and at times interchangeably in English. We know from Scripture that land belongs to God (see Leviticus 25:23–24; Exodus 9:29,19:5; Deuteronomy 10:12–14; Psalm 24:1). *Land* is the ground we walk on and build upon — the earth — the soil.

However, *world* is the cosmos — the spiritual realm around us, composed of spiritual systems and structures. Scripture makes it clear that this is the realm in which the enemy of God's people has his domain (see John 14:30; Ephesians 2:1–2; 1 John 5:19).

> 1 Samuel 2:8 distinguishes between the two realms — *"For the foundations of the **earth** are the Lord's; on them He has set the **world**."*

What is important to understand is that the enemy and his demonic realm can only access those areas in our lives — and what is on the land — through sin which has provided a **foothold** and becomes his access point.

When sin has not been addressed, then that foothold becomes **his right of access** here on earth. We then experience the consequences of that sin (cf. Chapter 4) which gives the enemy leverage in our lives and society — affecting whatever is on land.

What Do *You* See?

Old Testament prophets such as Jeremiah and Amos were frequently challenged with the question: *"What do you see?"* (Jeremiah 1:13; Amos 7:8, 8:2; Zechariah 4:2) in order to reveal God's intent for His people.

The New Testament instructs us to have the eyes of our heart enlightened (see Ephesians 1:17–19). The writer to the Hebrews challenges us in our understanding of faith — *"Now faith is confidence in what we hope for and assurance about what we do not see."* (Hebrews 11:1)

In Revelation 4, Jesus invites John to reposition his thinking and understanding in order to see and understand things from a different perspective — *"Come up here, and I will show you what must take place after this"* (vs. 1).

Seeing Clearly

In the past I had astigmatism and myopia in both eyes. I needed to wear corrective lenses for many years in order to see clearly. In due course I went through a form of laser treatment that corrected the cornea in both eyes which were too round and did not refract light properly. During the surgery, the cornea in both eyes were re-formed in order that light would refract correctly, and I was able to see without any need of corrective lenses. But what was really fascinating was that the *same* amount of light was still entering both eyes both before and after the procedure, but now I was seeing differently. A correction — a removal of "impediments" — had taken place in order for me to see clearly. I now had clear vision, physically.

Through this the Lord was illustrating to us the importance of "seeing" spiritually, without any impediments blurring the vision of His people. As we learned through the experience in our church, God wanted to change the corporate vision both within the church family — but also beyond the church into the wider community.

This is where 2 Corinthians 4:4 holds a clue for us —

"The god of this age has blinded the minds of unbelievers, so that they cannot see the light of the gospel that displays the glory of Christ, who is the image of God. "

We had a small but faithful fellowship of believers, yet our various attempts at evangelism, and our trying to live out the Kingdom of God yielded little fruit. What was missing? What was God trying to teach us? Could a corporate community actually have limited spiritual vision and have spiritually deafened ears towards the Kingdom message — and if so, could this be reversed?

If my physical vision had been distorted and was correctable, was this also correctable in the spiritual realm? Could we see what these obstacles and impediments might involve, and if so, could they be removed? Our leadership became excited! A powerful principle concerning the Kingdom of God began to grasp our attention.

A Distortion in our Worldview

There was a clear spiritual parallel in all this. We can be limited in what we perceive to be real based on what we physically see. We are not normally taught in this day and age to *see spiritually*, and this in itself has a huge influence upon the way that we pray. The challenge for much of Christendom these days is in learning to see and listen to the counsel of the Lord, as opposed to what our various areas of "learned observation" in the physical realm may otherwise try and tell us.

Our "worldview" influences the way we interpret reality and truth. Much of Western society is affected by the influence of **dualism** which separates the spiritual from the physical, the divine from the temporal. This is not a Biblical teaching and brings about a limited or distorted worldview in today's Church and in society as a whole.

Simply put, we often miss the vital truth that what we physically see around us is so often the result of what is spiritually going on around us. No-one can see wind — but we can readily see and feel the effect of it. Similarly, no-one can actually see "sin" — but we can all physically see the *effects* of sin. It's just that we are not generally taught to think in this manner — and yet, it is what reality is all about according to Scripture.

Recalibrating our Spiritual Sight and Hearing

Our spiritual eyes therefore need to be able to see what the Holy Spirit is wanting to reveal to us, just as our spiritual hearing must be in tune with what He is saying — a repeated theme in the Book of Revelation — *"Whoever has ears, let them hear what the Spirit says to the churches"* (Revelation 2:29,3:13,3:22).

Our worldview, which differs nation to nation, determines how we perceive our culture — our families — our societies — our education — our morals and ethics — our religion and spirituality — even global economics and finances — as well as marketing — industry and politics. A Kingdom of God worldview, however, is one in which the rule and reign of God influences how we think and respond and pray into all these areas.

Isaiah 32 reminds us that the Kingdom of God is a Kingdom in which *"the eyes of those who*

> Our "worldview" influences the way we interpret reality and truth.

see will no longer be closed, and the ears of those who hear will listen" (vs.3).

As we asked the Lord to open our eyes and ears to what He wanted to reveal to us about our community, we began to "see" in a new way, a Kingdom way. Addressing the historical and present-day issues through prayer, the community began to change, and new people began visiting our church who had never "seen" it before. When the access point or foothold of the enemy was addressed, healing came to that specific area both in and beyond the church. Our congregation experienced a five-fold growth in one year, yet we had no evangelism programme. We were simply obedient to God in this type of prayer and He was the Evangelist! The impediments were identified and removed — and seeds were now being sown that began to reap a harvest.

CHAPTER 4
The Defilements

On one occasion we were asked to visit an area of Atlantic Canada in which fish productivity had ceased and relationships between people were estranged. Leaders found it challenging to work with each other and issues of fear and competitiveness seemed to permeate the region. After prayer and research, it was found that specific sins had occurred here historically which significantly affected life and work in the area. There had been a legacy of idolatry and broken promises, as well as bloodshed and murder that had occurred between neighbouring groups of early inhabitants. There was a barrenness that seemed to affect the land, the people, and even the productivity of the sea.

After the prayer strategy was undertaken, major change occurred including the return of fish necessary for the industry of the area, and leadership and family relationships began to be restored. God was showing the direct connection between sins of the past which would still affect the present-day life in that area. It was exactly as promised in Scripture!

The Bible outlines four main classifications of sin that affect the land, as well as the people and structures and systems that exist upon the land in any given area. We will briefly examine all four, and then place them in a twenty-first century context —

1. Idolatry
(Exodus 20:3–5; Jeremiah 3:6–10, 16:18)

Scripture teaches that worshipping anyone or anything other than God is idolatry! This includes placing trust and faith and confidence in anyone other than God, even in the **gifting of others and self**! If idolatry exists in a certain area historically, the **worship of creation** will often take precedence over the worship of the Creator.

It can also include the **worship of the form and history** of the church and its programmes, if the subtle belief is that God can only work in that particular way!

2. Immorality and Fornication
(Leviticus 18:1–23; Romans 1:24–27)

Scripture is clear concerning various forms of sexuality and perversion that result in defilement of the land and its people. When issues such as these are not addressed, the **Church loses its God-given authority** as His prophetic voice on earth since it has compromised on a non-negotiable issue.

It can release a **lust for power** and **recognition**. The church is similar to a 'litmus test' that reveals the reality of what is going in a community. Often the toxic issues of sin must first be addressed within the church if it is going to have genuine authority to address it within the community.

This area of defilement can also be recognized when the church **lacks the humility and servant spirit** as seen in the life of Christ — a lack of wanting to pick up the towel and minister to the needs of others without seeking recognition or status.

3. Untimely Bloodshed
(Numbers 35:33–34; Isaiah 59:2–3)

Bloodshed is usually expressed in any aspect of murder and sacrifice. Within certain communities this is the root issue behind on-going crime. When not addressed, the 'fruit' of this defilement, even within a church, can be found lying behind such characteristics as

> Criticism
> Anger
> Jealousy
> Bitterness
> Rage (even if contained in the heart and not verbally spoken!)

4. Broken Covenants
(Isaiah 24:5–6)

This Scripture is quite explicit — *"The earth is defiled by its people; they have disobeyed the laws, violated the statutes and broken the everlasting covenant. Therefore, a curse consumes the earth; its people must bear their guilt..."*

The consequences of breaking covenant with God are vast and seen throughout Scripture. An unaddressed broken covenant between people and God — and people and people — at any level — can result in **on-going promises being broken**...

> Within staff and leadership relationships...
> Within marriage...
> Within families...
> Within the church body...

> Within the community...
> Within a city... and
> Even at national levels.

God is a God of covenant and promise and when this depth of relationship with God is broken, the protection, direction, provision, and intervention of God in all aspects of society can be removed since it has been a choice made by the people.

CHAPTER 5
The Consequences

We were asked to speak at a leaders' conference in a Caribbean nation. Following the conference, several leaders asked us to take a field trip to a specific area well-known in the nation. The problem was that the cattle and the people were always ill when living on this particular piece of land — but when moved to another area, they were fine. No productive harvest ever occurred on this particular piece of property. One could tangibly experience a sense of fear and apprehension that seemed to affect the entire area. God was revealing the consequences of past issues that had never been addressed which involved idolatry, bloodshed and betrayal. With the landowner, and local representatives, there was a time of prayer and repentance and re-dedication of land. This was maintained (stewarded) in the weeks following our departure. New growth in harvests, livestock, and a sense

Scripture is clear. When the relationship with God is broken, there are consequences.

of peace came upon the land. The old had gone and the new had begun.

Scripture is clear. When the relationship with God is broken, there are **consequences**. While society in general may have grown accustomed to a life in which the intervention and Presence of God is not necessarily looked for or experienced, nevertheless, it is wise that we see what these consequences involve. This enables us to see from God's point of view and to understand why certain things seem to exist or occur in one area, but reality in a neighbouring area can be quite different.

Ezekiel 14 is one passage that refers to all four consequences, or judgements, each having many different variations depending on the circumstances unique to our communities.

1. Famine
(Ezekiel 14:13; Amos 8:11)

The issue of **famine** speaks for itself in that there is an **absence of growth and productivity** upon the land necessary for sustaining life in that area. But the consequence of famine also enables us to determine earlier sins that may have occurred, and which need to be identified and addressed, especially when this famine is not just food-based.

When using the church as a litmus test, famine can be expressed as both **physical and spiritual hunger** that is never satisfied. It can be:

A hunger for **identity and purpose.**

A hunger for the **Presence of God**.

A hunger for **meaningful relationships** that never seem to be fulfilled between God and people — and between the people themselves.

A **famine of experiencing little harvest** in the lives of the people, even after a great deal of ministry and effort is undertaken.

2. Ecological Devastation

(Ezekiel 14:15; Jeremiah 23:10; Deuteronomy 11:17; Amos 4:7; Haggai 1:9–11)

This refers to much sowing but little harvesting both in the lives of people and in the land itself. Jeremiah 23:10 describes it in these graphic words — *"The land is full of adulterers; because of the curse the land lies parched and the pastures in the wilderness are withered..."* If we ignore God, it will affect all of life as we experience it.

Haggai 1:9 describes this in detail — *"'You expected much, but see, it turned out to be little. What you brought home, I blew away. Why?' declares the Lord Almighty. 'Because of My house, which remains a ruin, while each of you is busy with his own house.'"*

When using the church as a litmus test, ecological devastation can be experienced as:

Much work being done but yielding very little lasting fruit.

Vision that never seems to be fulfilled.

Almost reaching a goal — but never quite making it

The Church needs never quite being met

Constant fund-raising to meet essential bills

Repairs to the building requiring more time and attention than outreach into the community

3. War

(Ezekiel 14:17)

As well as political war between nations, there is also an *expression of war* in anger, jealousy, resentment, and competitiveness in society and in the church. It is the opposite of the type of unity we see demonstrated within the Godhead (see John 17) and described in Psalm 133 when those who live together in unity fulfill what is required for God to bestow (command) His blessing (see Psalm 133:3).

Assault can be verbal, physical, or relational toward an individual, a group, or a nation. A community may experience abnormal amounts of certain types of crime in specific areas.

When using the church as a litmus test, war can be expressed as unhealthy relationships, or a lack of trust and possible estrangement affecting —

Family members

Pastor and people

People and people

The worship team and the rest of the leadership team

Such divisions result in a lack of trust within staff relationships and a lack of unanimity in important decision-making.

4. Disease

(Ezekiel 14:19–20)

When a community, city, or nation is ravaged by disease, it is highly possible that at some point in history there has been an open door of defilement in that area.

But there can also be 'dis-ease'. Psalm 103 reminds us that God both forgives sins and heals all diseases, which can be physical, but also relational, mental, and emotional. A person and a community can both experience dis-ease. Psalm 32:3–4 describes life that groans and wastes away when sin is not addressed. But when it is addressed, forgiveness occurs, and sin is no longer counted against us (see Psalm 32:1–2,5).

Whether physical or spiritual, a defilement may have occurred which has given the enemy of God's people a foothold and "legal access" to that area.

When using the church as a litmus test, disease can be expressed as on-going physical illness that seems to affect the church family.

A sense of restlessness or unease or dissatisfaction within the church fellowship.

Areas within the community where there may be an emphasis of a specific type of physical illness.

Areas within the community where there is depression or sense of anxiety and sorrow — and little or no productivity

A Farm is Radically Changed

We were asked by a farmer if we could pray on his property and try to discover why his cattle were usually sick, why there were estrangements within family members, and why the land as a whole was so unproductive. He was a Christian and sought the Lord fervently looking for breakthrough — but little change was ever experienced.

After giving him some suggestions for research, he found through his family history, that earlier bestiality (people having sex with cattle) had occurred upon the land. This would have affected both the people who owned the land — as well as the livestock. After repentant prayer for all these activities a significant change came to the farm. The cattle became healthy and young calves were sold at market, yielding the highest price the market had ever seen — thus removing the debt on the farm. The productivity of the land itself changed, yielding healthy crops — the relationships of the family were restored — and new adjacent farmland was purchased expanding the boundaries of the farm.

The **sins** had been recognized and addressed. The **consequences** of the sin had affected the people and the entire farm for many years. Once the ministry had been undertaken there was **tangible healing** at all levels of life!

CHAPTER 6
Addressing the Land

A steward is someone responsible for someone else's property — in this case God's property (see Leviticus 25:23–24). We are here as God's stewards in order to bring the land back into relationship with Him. Having just looked at the subject of sin and defilement upon the land, and the consequences that can follow, we need to understand how to pray with insight and understanding.

Ephesians 4:27 holds a key — *"...and do not give the devil a foothold."* The word "foothold" in Greek is *topon* (from *topos*) and means a point of access or position that is given to Satan due to sin that has occurred, but which has not been addressed. It is a word that forms the basis of the English word **topographical**, a word used in cartographic — or mapping — circles.

Entry Points for the Demonic
Knowing how the enemy gains access through past and present sin becomes key for a breakthrough! Remember that he only gets access through sin by:

    What We ourselves do

What Others have done to us and how we responded or reacted in an ungodly way

The Influence of those who have gone before us, either in our ancestral lineage or those who may have occupied an office of responsibility before us

Those in position prior to us leave a defilement because of their sin and that defilement now has access to our lives (until it is identified and removed). We will experience the conflict of two Kingdoms since we are the centre point of that activity!

Some of these access points include:

At the Personal Level — lifestyle — culture — work — habits — and whatever we influence on earth.

At the Generational Level — recognizing the legacy of positive and negative actions in our family in past generations.

Within Offices of Responsibility — within the church — business — government.

Through corporate assent in which a community or group of people make a collective pact that is in opposition to the purposes of God.

Through the land itself and any buildings upon the land which may contain the "spiritual DNA" of past owners, based on what they did.

Through trauma, both personal and corporate, and how this may have affected an entire area such as a corporate circumstance that impacted an entire community.

The Power of the Tongue — both blessing and cursing are released in any area by the way we speak (see Proverbs 18:21; James 3:9)

Spiritual Warfare

Spiritual warfare is a reality in the twenty-first century church, and the basic aim of all spiritual authority is to break and remove any foothold or access the enemy has in our lives — our families — our churches — our businesses — our communities — our cities — and even our nations. This is in order for the power and authority of the Lord to regain through us, as His stewards, whatever was lost, hidden or stolen from earlier generations.

In this way, the enemy can no longer blind the eyes and minds of the people in that area (see 2 Corinthians 4:4). His right of access has been removed. The Presence of the Lord is released, and the land is healed, and His eyes and ears are opened and attentive to the prayers made in that place (see 2 Chronicles 7:14–15).

Generational Sins

It is key to remember that the Old Testament was the Bible for those who lived in the early New Testament days. What was foundational in the Old Testament was just as foundational in the New Testament — especially after the Cross. Land issues still affect us — only we now have the power and authority of the Cross to appropriate into each area of our responsibility as led by the Holy Spirit. In the words of Jesus Himself —

"Do not think that I have come to abolish the Law or the Prophets; I have not come to abolish them but to fulfill them. For truly I tell you, until heaven and earth disappear, not the smallest letter, not the least stroke of a pen, will by any means disappear from the Law until everything is accomplished." (Matthew 5:17–18) We need to remember that we reap what we sow — even in the spiritual realm! Proverbs 22:8 states: *"Whoever sows injustice reaps calamity..."* Paul makes this clear in Galatians 6:7–8

"Do not be deceived; God cannot be mocked. A man reaps what he sows. Whoever sows to please their flesh, from the flesh will

reap destruction; whoever sows to please the Spirit, from the Spirit will reap eternal life. "

We, therefore, can easily be the recipients of whatever was sown in past generations — both bad and good, which both the Old and New Testaments confirm:

> Deuteronomy 28:58–59 — *"If you do not carefully follow all the words of this law, which are written in this book, and do not revere this glorious and awesome name — the Lord your God — the Lord will send fearful plagues on you and your descendants, harsh and prolonged disasters and severe and lingering diseases…"*

Matthew 23:35–36 — *"And so upon you will come all the righteous blood that has been shed on earth, from the blood of righteous Abel to the blood of Zechariah… Truly I tell you, all this will come on this generation."*

Spiritual Sewers and Drains

Blocked drains are annoying, and they tend to appear often with little warning! Usually there is a blockage somewhere in the draining system under the sink, or it may be that the main drainage system has become clogged or choked with roots and other obstructions under the surface of the soil. Then a more thorough form of de-clogging is required.

> At times we may need to gain access to a city through the stench and smell of sin that has defiled the land.

In 2 Samuel 5, we read that David has now been anointed king of Israel and he wants to regain possession of Jerusalem. The Jebusites currently occupied the city and ridiculed David and his men saying it was impossible for them to enter Jerusalem.

But David had a strategy and his men were able to enter the city through the water shaft (see 2 Samuel 5:8). The water shaft would be the equivalent to the drain or sewers of the day, and for this reason the enemy never thought this would become their place of vulnerability. Not only was the enemy defeated — the city was returned to the Lord!

Uncover — Discover — Recover

In other words, at times we may need to gain access to a city through the stench and smell of sin that has defiled the land. We are addressing whatever issues have given the enemy access. Such issues will reflect the lives and work of those who have lived there over the years, which is why we undertake any necessary research and see from God's point of view what is really at stake. God's strategy is profound —

> He will **uncover** for us what is at the heart of the issues.

> He will enable us to **discover** what is separating the people from Him.

> He will give us the keys to **recover** His destiny and healing for the people and the land.

We have to be willing to address the issue of entrenched religion — or shame — or offense — broken covenants — or injustice — or anger — or unforgiveness — or depression and disappointment — or loss and loneliness, or whatever He reveals. To the degree we address whatever these spiritual sewers of our communities may contain, to that same degree we can expect to see breakthrough in that area as the eyes and ears of the people are opened to the Presence of the Lord. Then we will see His healing on the land.

This was the breakthrough for our church.

Remedy — The Power of Forgiveness and Repentance

An offence upon the land may not have occurred as a result of our actions or in our present time. This is an occasion when we stand in the gap — the place of responsibility — and confess whatever sins have to be addressed — and offer whatever forgiveness is required. Through the power of repentance, whatever is contrary to God's plan for His people can be reversed and the land can be healed. In other words, the defiling state of affairs upon the land which has affected the spiritual realm with consequent flow-on to the productivity of the people and the area is now being remedied.

Through representing our sphere of activity and work, we can identify with whatever sins need to be addressed, and address each area of access in a community, as referred to in our book *God's Design for Challenging Times*. These access points — or doorways — are part of the land and all hold a key to the destiny of that place which God wants to release since He is a covenantal God of promise.

Understanding the generational aspect of what we are doing, we are choosing to see the need for repentance from God's point of view and not from any sense of human justification or compromise. Remember we are wanting to dismiss any legal right the enemy has in that place which may well have influenced the spiritual realm in that area. We are seeking to determine what has offended God.

Nehemiah 1:3–9 reveals the extent by which the sin had devastated Nehemiah since it had all but spiritually paralyzed the people of the land in their relationship with God. The wall of Jerusalem was broken, and its gates burned with fire (see Nehemiah 1:3). He fasted and prayed and then declared —

> *"I confess the sins we Israelites, including myself and my father's house, have committed against You. We have acted*

very wickedly toward You. We have not obeyed the commands, decrees and laws You gave Your servant Moses." (Nehemiah 1:6b–7)

Similarly, Ezra states —

"I am too ashamed and disgraced, my God, to lift up my face to you, because our sins are higher than our heads and our guilt has reached to the heavens." (Ezra 9:6)

> We need to remember that God is timeless and therefore multi-generational.

This offense had affected the land — *"...The land you are entering to possess is a land polluted by the corruption of its peoples. By their detestable practices they have filled it with their impurity from one end to the other."* (Ezra 9:11)

Taking Responsibility
We can take responsibility for what has been done by anyone we represent based on:

Our race

Our office of responsibility (our portfolio)

Our culture

Our affiliation (denomination, membership in an organization)

Our gender

Sometimes our age (for example when grandparents are repenting towards grandchildren — and vice versa).

We need to remember that God is timeless and therefore multi-generational. The impact of our prayer of repentance is much more than simply saying: "we are sorry." Rather it is an ownership of responsibility — and we become the generation **NOW** that will turn from the ways of the past.

We are representing those before us who have brought offense to the Lord which has affected the land. We are, therefore, willing to seek whatever **restitution** may be required to remove the offense from the land (we are removing the foothold). On behalf of those before us, we are now separating ourselves from any wickedness and rebellion before the Lord — and choosing to return to Him in order that His Presence and Purpose will rest in our midst (see 2 Chronicles 6:40–41, 7:16; Isaiah 33:10; Psalm 12:5, 132:8).

Results of Repentance
I want it back!

On one occasion, our team was asked to pray through a prominent city church. Although it appeared to be a "successful" church, the Pastor told us of several struggles with finances, worship, tradition, and various groups vying for control. Unholy influence affected the decision-making. After a time of prayer and repentance and addressing the strongholds that were affecting their church life, there was a distinct change in the atmosphere. The following morning, the pastor had a visitor — a well-known fortune teller — who said she had lost her power the previous night (exactly during the time of repentance and prayer in the church) and that she wanted it back since she could no longer work without this power. The sin and defilement within the church had empowered her influence, but now that had been removed. The pastor denied her request!

> When repentance is prayed, we are affected now!
> It restores our intimacy with God and removes any sense of separation in our relationship with Him.

Within a short time, the individuals in the church who had been obstructive and confrontational, quietly resigned from their duties. These changes came not through confrontation but solely from strategic prayer. The church entered a new season of growth and renewal that was experienced internally — but also externally in the community.

When repentance is prayed, we are affected now! It removes the consequence of former sins that have affected the present. God will arise and come to us now — His "resting place". It restores our intimacy with God and removes any sense of separation in our relationship with Him. It allows His love, His direction in our lives, and His healing in our midst to be applied in the lives of the people and upon the land. It stops the legal right of the enemy to accuse and intimidate any longer, and it releases God's destiny upon His people and upon the generations that follow (see Exodus 23:20–31; Deuteronomy 28:1–14).

CHAPTER 7
The Land is Healed

2 Chronicles 7:14 gives insight to the requirements required for healing the land. The Hebrew word being used for "heal" is *rapha* which means "to cause to heal". Literally, it means to **heal — mend —** and **repair** and to bring about **wholeness**. This is a word synonymous with medical doctors and it implies that, just as a medical physician brings healing to a person, similarly the Lord promises to bring healing to His land once the people have addressed any and all fallen stewardship in their midst. It is a powerful promise coming from the heart of the Godhead.

As described in detail in our book, *In Holy Fear*, prayer on the land may include prophetic acts using water, salt and oil, Communion using bread and wine, staking the land, and releasing the canopy of the Lord over that area. There is no "power" in the objects themselves but when used under the direction of the Holy Spirit, they become part of the prayer strategy for the land and water as we pray for the return of health and productivity to that area (see Exodus 15:22–27; 2 Kings 2:19–22).

The Blessings

Leviticus 26 is an early summary in Scripture that reveals God's intent for His people. Here we are given a list of what we can expect to receive in our relationship with God once the land has been redeemed. These can best be described as the blessings that come from obedience which are repeated throughout Scripture.

1. **Ecological health** — *"I will send you rain in its season, and the ground will yield its crops and the trees their fruit"* (Leviticus 26:4). This is a promise for an increase in natural resources and shifting from drought to showers of blessing. We have watched miraculous shifts especially within farming communities when their land is healed. We have recorded many examples of a minimization of natural disasters, and an increase in productivity.

2. **Economic Health** — *"Your threshing will continue until grape harvest and the grape harvest will continue until planting, and you will eat all the food you want and live in safety in your land"* (Leviticus 26:5). This is a promise for an increase in our harvest and commodities within business and a wisdom in handling economics.

3. **Personal Security** — *"I will grant peace in the land, and you will lie down and no one will make you afraid"* (Leviticus 26:6a). This is a promise for a lower crime rate, a removal of "neighbourhood fear", a reduction of dissension between people on the land and a removal of general unrest (see Psalm 144:14).

4. **Civil Security** — *"I will remove savage beasts from the land, and the sword will not pass through your country"* (Leviticus 26:6b). This is a promise for addressing corruption and hidden agendas in society, and an increased protection in our corporate life and work.

5. **International Security** — *"You will pursue your enemies, and they will fall by the sword before you. Five of you will chase a hundred, and a hundred of you will chase ten thousand"* (Leviticus 26:7-8a). This promises a new authority over any challenges and impediments to God's vision, one in which our weakness is replaced with His strength. Then His Presence, His Provision and Protection will dwell on the land with His people.

6. **Honour and Growth** — *"I will look on you with favor and make you fruitful and increase your numbers, and I will keep my covenant with you"* (Leviticus 26:9). God's promise is to visit the land and release His favour on our productivity and release and extend His purpose for His people and the land.

7. **Innovation and Creativity** — *"You will still be eating last year's harvest when you will have to move it out to make room for the new"* (Leviticus 26:10). This is His promise for untapped resources, creativity and riches that will now be released, both individually and corporately, in our midst.

After citing these blessings that come from obedience, Leviticus 26:11–13 then describes what happens when the Presence of the Lord comes and dwells with His people —

"I will put My dwelling place among you, and I will not abhor you. I will walk among you and be your God, and you will be My people. I am the Lord your God, who brought you out of Egypt so that you would no longer be slaves to the Egyptians; I broke the bars

Land is the meeting place between God and man. Whatever has taken place upon land is of key consequence to Him.

*of your yoke and enabled you to walk **with heads held high**."* (emphasis mine)

Land is the meeting place between God and man. Whatever has taken place upon land is of key consequence to Him. He is jealous for His land (see Joel 2:18), and He is also a holy God that will not allow His Presence to be mixed with unholiness and compromise.

In this book we have looked at some of the Biblical principles of stewardship that, when applied with prayer and diligence, releases the power and authority of the Kingdom of heaven on earth and prepares the way for the return of the Bridegroom. Yet as we have also seen there are Biblical parameters we must respect and appropriate if we are to experience God's glory in our lives, in our communities, in our nations — indeed, upon our land. Right from the earliest days of recorded biblical history God could be heard walking in the Garden (c.f. Genesis 3:8) — indicative of His desire for His Presence to be in our midst — and His Footprint to be on the land.

"O Land, land, land, hear the word of the Lord!" (Jeremiah 22:29)

ENDNOTES

1.	*God's Design for Challenging Times* by Rev. Dr. Alistair Petrie — Page 108–110 — Published by CHI-Books, PO Box 6462, Upper Mount Gravatt, QLD 4122 Australia. ISBN 978-0-9870891-0-6.

2.	*In Holy Fear* by Rev. Dr. Alistair Petrie — Page 91–95 — Published by CHI-Books, PO Box 6462, Upper Mount Gravatt, QLD 4122 Australia. ISBN 978-0-9942607-2-7.

3.	*Releasing Heaven on Earth* by Rev. Dr. Alistair Petrie — Page 190–199 — Published by Sovereign World, PO Box 784, Ellel, Lancaster LA1 9DA, England. ISBN 978-1-85240-481-9 *(Currently out of print).*
	Copies of our workbook — *A Sacred Trust* — containing this information may be ordered directly from Partnership Ministries — www.partnershipministries.org or downloaded from our website.

ABOUT THE AUTHOR

Rev. Dr Alistair P. Petrie

For many years in both the United Kingdom and Canada, Alistair served as senior pastor in diverse city church settings. With that experience and his earlier years spent in professional broadcasting, he now serves as the Executive Director of Partnership Ministries, a global ministry that teaches the principles and relevance of the Gospel and its relationship to the wider Church, the Marketplace, to Cities and to Nations. Partnership Ministries is positioned as a ministry for the 21st Century Church and combines prayer and research to prepare for lasting revival, authentic transformation and the release of Kingdom culture. In doing so, Alistair consults regularly with churches and ministries, businesses, and business leaders helping them in applying the principles of Transformation in their areas of influence — and explains how this releases cities and nations into their respective destinies.

Alistair has travelled extensively to many nations researching and teaching these transformation principles, in both church and city settings as well as in the marketplace arena. Obtaining his Doctorate through Fuller Seminary, he has been a guest lecturer at several academic settings and Schools of Ministry. As well as being an international speaker, he is the author of several books, and along with his ministry team has produced an informative DVD teaching series. He is married to Marie and they have two married children.

For more information on Partnership Ministries regarding their tools, training resources and webinars, please visit their website.

www.partnershipministries.org

CPSIA information can be obtained
at www.ICGtesting.com
Printed in the USA
BVHW040318060221
599326BV00006B/11

9 780648 510857